MznLnx

Missing Links Exam Preps

Exam Prep for

Creative Management in Recreation, Parks, and Leisure Services

Kraus & Curtis, 6th Edition

The MznLnx Exam Prep is your link from the texbook and lecture to your exams.
The MznLnx Exam Preps are unauthorized and comprehensive reviews of your textbooks.

All material provided by MznLnx and Rico Publications (c) 2010
Textbook publishers and textbook authors do not particpate in or contribute to these reviews.

MznLnx

Rico
Publications

Exam Prep for Creative Management in Recreation, Parks, and Leisure Services
6th Edition
Kraus & Curtis

Publisher: Raymond Houge
Assistant Editor: Michael Rouger
Text and Cover Designer: Lisa Buckner
Marketing Manager: Sara Swagger
Project Manager, Editorial Production: Jerry Emerson
Art Director: Vernon Lowerui

Product Manager: Dave Mason
Editorial Assitant: Rachel Guzmanji
Pedagogy: Debra Long
Cover Image: Jim Reed/Getty Images
Text and Cover Printer: City Printing, Inc.
Compositor: Media Mix, Inc.

(c) 2010 Rico Publications

ALL RIGHTS RESERVED. No part of this work covered by the copyright may be reproduced or used in any form or by an means--graphic, electronic, or mechanical, including photocopying, recording, taping, Web distribution, information storage, and retrieval systems, or in any other manner--without the written permission of the publisher.

Printed in the United States
ISBN:

For more information about our products, contact us at:
Dave.Mason@RicoPublications.com

For permission to use material from this text or product, submit a request online to:
Dave.Mason@RicoPublications.com

Contents

CHAPTER 1
Managers in the Leisure-Service System — 1

CHAPTER 2
Management as a Professional Discipline — 6

CHAPTER 3
Key Management Roles in Leisure-Service Agencies — 13

CHAPTER 4
Leisure-Service Program Development — 18

CHAPTER 5
Facilities Development and Maintenance — 22

CHAPTER 6
Creative Fiscal Management — 27

CHAPTER 7
Human Resource Management: Maximizing Staff Performance — 37

CHAPTER 8
Public and Community Relations: Growing Use of Partnerships — 46

CHAPTER 9
Leisure Services and the Law: Risk-Management Concerns — 49

CHAPTER 10
The Controlling Function — 56

CHAPTER 11
The Creative Manager: Facing the Future — 61

ANSWER KEY — 67

TO THE STUDENT

COMPREHENSIVE

The *MznLnx* Exam Prep series is designed to help you pass your exams. Editors at MznLnx review your textbooks and then prepare these practice exams to help you master the textbook material. Unlike study guides, workbooks, and practice tests provided by the texbook publisher and textbook authors, *MznLnx* gives you **all** of the material in each chapter in exam form, not just samples, so you can be sure to nail your exam.

MECHANICAL

The MznLnx Exam Prep series creates exams that will help you learn the subject matter as well as test you on your understanding. Each question is designed to help you master the concept. Just working through the exams, you gain an understanding of the subject--its a simple mechanical process that produces success.

INTEGRATED STUDY GUIDE AND REVIEW

MznLnx is not just a set of exams designed to test you, its also a comprehensive review of the subject content. Each exam question is also a review of the concept, making sure that you will get the answer correct without having to go to other sources of material. You learn as you go! Its the easiest way to pass an exam.

HUMOR

Studying can be tedious and dry. MznLnx's instructional design includes moderate humor within the exam questions on occassion, to break the tedium and revitalize the brain

Chapter 1. Managers in the Leisure-Service System

1. _____ is a national organization whose mission is to 'enable all young people, especially those who need us most, to reach their full potential as productive, caring, responsible citizens.' Club programs and services promote and enhance the development of boys and girls by instilling a sense of competence, usefulness, belonging and influence.

Headquarters are located in Atlanta, with regional offices in Chicago, Dallas, Atlanta, New York City and Los Angeles.

The group holds a congressional charter under Title 36 of the United States Code.

   a. Wells Fargo ' Co.
   b. Boys ' Girls Clubs of America
   c. National Association of Corporate Directors
   d. National Association for the Advancement of Colored People

2. A _____ is a type of business entity in which partners (owners) share with each other the profits or losses of the business. _____s are often favored over corporations for taxation purposes, as the _____ structure does not generally incur a tax on profits before it is distributed to the partners (i.e. there is no dividend tax levied.) However, depending on the _____ structure and the jurisdiction in which it operates, owners of a _____ may be exposed to greater personal liability than they would as shareholders of a corporation.

   a. Partnership
   b. Due process
   c. Mediation
   d. Federal Employers Liability Act

3. _____ is an advertisement in which a particular product specifically mentions a competitor by name for the express purpose of showing why the competitor is inferior to the product naming it.

This should not be confused with parody advertisements, where a fictional product is being advertised for the purpose of poking fun at the particular advertisement, nor should it be confused with the use of a coined brand name for the purpose of comparing the product without actually naming an actual competitor. ('Wikipedia tastes better and is less filling than the Encyclopedia Galactica.')

In the 1980s, during what has been referred to as the cola wars, soft-drink manufacturer Pepsi ran a series of advertisements where people, caught on hidden camera, in a blind taste test, chose Pepsi over rival Coca-Cola.

   a. 1990 Clean Air Act
   b. 28-hour day
   c. 33 Strategies of War
   d. Comparative advertising

Chapter 1. Managers in the Leisure-Service System

4. The term '_____' refers to the concept of collecting information and attempting to spot a pattern in the information. In some fields of study, the term '_____' has more formally-defined meanings.

In project management _____ is a mathematical technique that uses historical results to predict future outcome.

   a. Trend analysis
   b. Regression analysis
   c. Least squares
   d. Stepwise regression

5. _____ is the point where a person stops employment completely. A person may also semi-retire and keep some sort of _____ job, out of choice rather than necessity. This usually happens upon reaching a determined age, when physical conditions don't allow the person to work any more (by illness or accident), or even for personal choice (usually in the presence of an adequate pension or personal savings.)
   a. Severance package
   b. Termination of employment
   c. Wrongful dismissal
   d. Retirement

6. An _____ is a comprehensive report on a company's activities throughout the preceding year. _____s are intended to give shareholders and other interested persons information about the company's activities and financial performance. Most jurisdictions require companies to prepare and disclose _____s, and many require the _____ to be filed at the company's registry.
   a. AAAI
   b. A Stake in the Outcome
   c. Annual report
   d. A4e

7. _____ is a term defined by the Oxford English Dictionary as an individual's 'course or progress through life '. It is usually considered to pertain to remunerative work (and sometimes also formal education.)

The etymology of the term is somewhat ironic in that it comes from the Latin word carrera, which means race .

   a. Spatial mismatch
   b. Career planning
   c. Career
   d. Nursing shortage

Chapter 1. Managers in the Leisure-Service System

8. In organizational development (or OD), the study of _____ looks at:

   - how individuals manage their careers within and between organizations
   - and how organizations structure the career progress of their members, it can also be tied into succession planning within some organizations.

In personal development, _____ is:

- ' ... the total constellation of psychological, sociological, educational, physical, economic, and chance factors that combine to influence the nature and significance of work in the total lifespan of any given individual.'

- '... the lifelong psychological and behavioral processes as well as contextual influences shaping one's career over the life span. As such, _____ involves the person's creation of a career pattern, decision-making style, integration of life roles, values expression, and life-role self concepts.'

Figures in _____

- Jeff A. Brown
- Jesse B. Davis
- Caela Farren
- John L. Holland
- Kris Magnusson
- Frank Parsons
- Vance Peavy
- Edgar Schein
- Rino Schreuder
- Mark L. Savickas
- Donald Super

a. Horizontal integration
b. Business process reengineering
c. Career development
d. Sole proprietorship

9. _____ is a recursive process where two or more people or organizations work together in an intersection of common goals -- for example, an intellectual endeavor that is creative in nature--by sharing knowledge, learning and building consensus. _____ does not require leadership and can sometimes bring better results through decentralization and egalitarianism. In particular, teams that work collaboratively can obtain greater resources, recognition and reward when facing competition for finite resources._____ is also present in opposing goals exhibiting the notion of adversarial _____, though this is not a common case for using the term.

a. 1990 Clean Air Act
   b. Collectivism
   c. 28-hour day
   d. Collaboration

10. _____ according to Onuoha (2007) is the practice of starting new organizations or revitalizing mature organizations, particularly new businesses generally in response to identified opportunities. _____ is often a difficult undertaking, as a vast majority of new businesses fail. Entrepreneurial activities are substantially different depending on the type of organization that is being started.
   a. Entrepreneurship
   b. A Stake in the Outcome
   c. AAAI
   d. A4e

11. An _____ is a mostly hierarchical concept of subordination of entities that collaborate and contribute to serve one common aim.

Organizations are a variant of clustered entities. The structure of an organization is usually set up in many a styles, dependent on their objectives and ambience.

   a. Informal organization
   b. Organizational development
   c. Open shop
   d. Organizational structure

12. _____ is a process for determining and addressing needs, or gaps between current conditions and desired conditions organizations it is known as community needs analysis. It involves identifying material problems/deficits/weaknesses and advantages/opportunites/strengths, and evaluating possible solutions that take those qualities into consideration.
   a. 1990 Clean Air Act
   b. 28-hour day
   c. 33 Strategies of War
   d. Needs assessment

13. A _____ is a list of the general tasks and responsibilities of a position. Typically, it also includes to whom the position reports, specifications such as the qualifications needed by the person in the job, salary range for the position, etc. A _____ is usually developed by conducting a job analysis, which includes examining the tasks and sequences of tasks necessary to perform the job.

a. Recruitment advertising
b. Recruitment
c. Recruitment Process Insourcing
d. Job description

14. The _____ of 1990 (ADA) is the short title of United States (Pub.L. 101-336, 104 Stat. 327, enacted July 26, 1990), codified at 42 U.S.C. § 12101 et seq. It was signed into law on July 26, 1990, by President George H. W. Bush, and later amended with changes effective January 1, 2009. The ADA is a wide-ranging civil rights law that prohibits, under certain circumstances, discrimination based on disability. It affords similar protections against discrimination to Americans with disabilities as the Civil Rights Act of 1964,
   a. Australian labour law
   b. Equal Pay Act of 1963
   c. Americans with Disabilities Act
   d. Employment discrimination

Chapter 2. Management as a Professional Discipline

1. _____ is one of the managerial functions like planning, organizing, staffing and directing. It is an important function because it helps to check the errors and to take the corrective action so that deviation from standards are minimized and stated goals of the organization are achieved in desired manner. According to modern concepts, _____ is a foreseeing action whereas earlier concept of _____ was used only when errors were detected. _____ in management means setting standards, measuring actual performance and taking corrective action.

   a. Decision tree pruning
   b. Turnover
   c. Schedule of reinforcement
   d. Control

2. An _____, or organogram(me)) is a diagram that shows the structure of an organization and the relationships and relative ranks of its parts and positions/jobs. The term is also used for similar diagrams, for example ones showing the different elements of a field of knowledge or a group of languages. The French Encyclopédie had one of the first _____s of knowledge in general.

   a. A Stake in the Outcome
   b. A4e
   c. Organizational chart
   d. AAAI

3. _____, widely known as F. W. Taylor, was an American mechanical engineer who sought to improve industrial efficiency. He is regarded as the father of scientific management, and was one of the first management consultants.

   Taylor was one of the intellectual leaders of the Efficiency Movement and his ideas, broadly conceived, were highly influential in the Progressive Era.

   a. Douglas N. Daft
   b. Jonah Jacob Goldberg
   c. Frederick Winslow Taylor
   d. Geoffrey Colvin

4. A _____ is a business efficiency technique combining the Time Study work of Frederick Winslow Taylor with the Motion Study work of Frank and Lillian Gilbreth (not to be confused with their son, best known through the biographical 1950 film and book Cheaper by the Dozen.) It is a major part of scientific management (Taylorism.)

   A _____ would be used to reduce the number of motions in performing a task in order to increase productivity.

Chapter 2. Management as a Professional Discipline

a. Prevailing wage
b. Total benefits of ownership
c. Time and motion study
d. Manufacturing operations

5. Organizational studies, organizational behaviour, and _____ is the systematic study and careful application of knowledge about how people - as individuals and as groups - act within organizations.

Organizational Behaviour studies encompasses the study of organizations from multiple viewpoints, methods, and levels of analysis. For instance, one textbook divides these multiple viewpoints into three perspectives: modern, symbolic, and postmodern.

a. Organizational theory
b. A Stake in the Outcome
c. A4e
d. AAAI

6. _____ Movement refers to those researchers of organizational development who study the behavior of people in groups, in particular workplace groups. It originated in the 1920s' Hawthorne studies, which examined the effects of social relations, motivation and employee satisfaction on factory productivity. The movement viewed workers in terms of their psychology and fit with companies, rather than as interchangeable parts.

a. Human relations
b. Participatory management
c. Work design
d. Hersey-Blanchard situational theory

7. An _____ is a mostly hierarchical concept of subordination of entities that collaborate and contribute to serve one common aim.

Organizations are a variant of clustered entities. The structure of an organization is usually set up in many a styles, dependent on their objectives and ambience.

a. Organizational structure
b. Open shop
c. Informal organization
d. Organizational development

Chapter 2. Management as a Professional Discipline

8. _____ and Theory Y are theories of human motivation created and developed by Douglas McGregor at the MIT Sloan School of Management in the 1960s that have been used in human resource management, organizational behavior, organizational communication and organizational development. They describe two very different attitudes toward workforce motivation. McGregor felt that companies followed either one or the other approach.

In _____, which many managers practice, management assumes employees are inherently lazy and will avoid work if they can. They inherently dislike work. Because of this, workers need to be closely supervised and comprehensive systems of controls developed.

   a. Management team
   b. Cash cow
   c. Theory X
   d. Job enrichment

9. Theory X and _____ are theories of human motivation created and developed by Douglas McGregor at the MIT Sloan School of Management in the 1960s that have been used in human resource management, organizational behavior, organizational communication and organizational development. They describe two very different attitudes toward workforce motivation. McGregor felt that companies followed either one or the other approach.

In _____, management assumes employees may be ambitious and self-motivated and exercise self-control. It is believed that employees enjoy their mental and physical work duties.

   a. Business Workflow Analysis
   b. Contingency theory
   c. Design leadership
   d. Theory Y

10. _____ has been described as the 'process of social influence in which one person can enlist the aid and support of others in the accomplishment of a common task'. A definition more inclusive of followers comes from Alan Keith of Genentech who said '_____ is ultimately about creating a way for people to contribute to making something extraordinary happen.'

_____ is one of the most salient aspects of the organizational context. However, defining _____ has been challenging.

   a. 1990 Clean Air Act
   b. 28-hour day
   c. Situational leadership
   d. Leadership

Chapter 2. Management as a Professional Discipline

11. _____ can be regarded as an outcome of mental processes (cognitive process) leading to the selection of a course of action among several alternatives. Every _____ process produces a final choice. The output can be an action or an opinion of choice.
    a. Decision making
    b. 28-hour day
    c. 1990 Clean Air Act
    d. 33 Strategies of War

12. _____ is a range of processes aimed at alleviating or eliminating sources of conflict. The term '_____' is sometimes used interchangeably with the term dispute resolution or alternative dispute resolution. Processes of _____ generally include negotiation, mediation and diplomacy.
    a. Conflict resolution
    b. 1990 Clean Air Act
    c. 33 Strategies of War
    d. 28-hour day

13. A _____ is a volunteer group composed of workers (or even students), usually under the leadership of their supervisor (but they can elect a team leader), who are trained to identify, analyse and solve work-related problems and present their solutions to management in order to improve the performance of the organization, and motivate and enrich the work of employees. When matured, true _____s become self-managing, having gained the confidence of management. _____s are an alternative to the dehumanising concept of the Division of Labour, where workers or individuals are treated like robots.
    a. Competency-based job descriptions
    b. Connectionist expert systems
    c. Certified in Production and Inventory Management
    d. Quality circle

14. _____ is an interdisciplinary field of science and the study of the nature of complex systems in nature, society, and science. More specifically, it is a framework by which one can analyze and/or describe any group of objects that work in concert to produce some result. This could be a single organism, any organization or society, or any electro-mechanical or informational artifact.
    a. 28-hour day
    b. Systems thinking
    c. 1990 Clean Air Act
    d. Systems theory

Chapter 2. Management as a Professional Discipline

15. _____ describes the situation when output from (or information about the result of) an event or phenomenon in the past will influence the same event/phenomenon in the present or future. When an event is part of a chain of cause-and-effect that forms a circuit or loop, then the event is said to 'feed back' into itself.

_____ is also a synonym for:

- _____ signal; the information about the initial event that is the basis for subsequent modification of the event.
- _____ loop; the causal path that leads from the initial generation of the _____ signal to the subsequent modification of the event.

_____ is a mechanism, process or signal that is looped back to control a system within itself. Such a loop is called a _____ loop.

a. Positive feedback
b. Feedback loop
c. 1990 Clean Air Act
d. Feedback

16. The _____, is a mathematically based algorithm for scheduling a set of project activities. It is an important tool for effective project management.

It was developed in the 1950s by the Dupont Corporation at about the same time that General Dynamics and the US Navy were developing the Program Evaluation and Review Technique (PERT) Today, it is commonly used with all forms of projects, including construction, software development, research projects, product development, engineering, and plant maintenance, among others.

a. 1990 Clean Air Act
b. 33 Strategies of War
c. Critical path method
d. 28-hour day

17. _____ is a business management strategy aimed at embedding awareness of quality in all organizational processes. _____ has been widely used in manufacturing, education, hospitals, call centers, government, and service industries, as well as NASA space and science programs.

Chapter 2. Management as a Professional Discipline

As defined by the International Organization for Standardization (ISO):

'_____ is a management approach for an organization, centered on quality, based on the participation of all its members and aiming at long-term success through customer satisfaction, and benefits to all members of the organization and to society.' ISO 8402:1994

One major aim is to reduce variation from every process so that greater consistency of effort is obtained. (Royse, D., Thyer, B., Padgett D., ' Logan T., 2006)

  a. 1990 Clean Air Act
  b. Quality management
  c. Total quality management
  d. 28-hour day

18. _____ is the process of comparing the cost, cycle time, productivity, or quality of a specific process or method to another that is widely considered to be an industry standard or best practice. Essentially, _____ provides a snapshot of the performance of your business and helps you understand where you are in relation to a particular standard. The result is often a business case for making changes in order to make improvements.

  a. Competitive heterogeneity
  b. Benchmarking
  c. Cost leadership
  d. Complementors

19. _____ of the learning curve effect and the closely related experience curve effect express the relationship between equations for experience and efficiency or between efficiency gains and investment in the effort. The experience of 'learning curves' was first observed by the 19th Century German psychologist Hermann Ebbinghaus according to the difficulty of memorizing varying numbers of verbal stimuli, and subsequent learning about the complex processes of learning are discussed in the

The rule used for representing the learning curve effect states that the more times a task has been performed, the less time will be required on each subsequent iteration.

  a. Point biserial correlation coefficient
  b. Distribution
  c. Spatial Decision Support Systems
  d. Models

Chapter 2. Management as a Professional Discipline

20. _____ can be considered to have three main components: quality control, quality assurance and quality improvement. _____ is focused not only on product quality, but also the means to achieve it. _____ therefore uses quality assurance and control of processes as well as products to achieve more consistent quality.

   a. 1990 Clean Air Act
   b. 28-hour day
   c. Quality management
   d. Total quality management

21. The term '_____' refers to the concept of collecting information and attempting to spot a pattern in the information. In some fields of study, the term '_____' has more formally-defined meanings.

In project management _____ is a mathematical technique that uses historical results to predict future outcome.

   a. Regression analysis
   b. Stepwise regression
   c. Least squares
   d. Trend analysis

22. _____ according to Onuoha (2007) is the practice of starting new organizations or revitalizing mature organizations, particularly new businesses generally in response to identified opportunities. _____ is often a difficult undertaking, as a vast majority of new businesses fail. Entrepreneurial activities are substantially different depending on the type of organization that is being started.

   a. A Stake in the Outcome
   b. AAAI
   c. Entrepreneurship
   d. A4e

Chapter 3. Key Management Roles in Leisure-Service Agencies

1. _____ is a national organization whose mission is to 'enable all young people, especially those who need us most, to reach their full potential as productive, caring, responsible citizens.' Club programs and services promote and enhance the development of boys and girls by instilling a sense of competence, usefulness, belonging and influence.

Headquarters are located in Atlanta, with regional offices in Chicago, Dallas, Atlanta, New York City and Los Angeles.

The group holds a congressional charter under Title 36 of the United States Code.

   a. Boys ' Girls Clubs of America
   b. National Association for the Advancement of Colored People
   c. Wells Fargo ' Co.
   d. National Association of Corporate Directors

2. A _____ is a brief written statement of the purpose of a company or organization. Ideally, a _____ guides the actions of the organization, spells out its overall goal, provides a sense of direction, and guides decision making for all levels of management.

_____s often contain the following:

   - Purpose and aim of the organization
   - The organization's primary stakeholders: clients, stockholders, etc.
   - Responsibilities of the organization toward these stakeholders
   - Products and services offered

In developing a _____:

   - Encourage as much input as feasible from employees, volunteers, and other stakeholders
   - Publicize it broadly

The _____ can be used to resolve differences between business stakeholders. Stakeholders include: employees including managers and executives, stockholders, board of directors, customers, suppliers, distributors, creditors, governments (local, state, federal, etc.), unions, competitors, NGO's, and the general public.

   a. 33 Strategies of War
   b. 28-hour day
   c. 1990 Clean Air Act
   d. Mission statement

3. A _____ is typically described as a deliberate plan of action to guide decisions and achieve rational outcome(s.) However, the term may also be used to denote what is actually done, even though it is unplanned.

Chapter 3. Key Management Roles in Leisure-Service Agencies

The term may apply to government, private sector organizations and groups, and individuals.

a. 28-hour day
b. Policy
c. 33 Strategies of War
d. 1990 Clean Air Act

4. A _____ is a type of business entity in which partners (owners) share with each other the profits or losses of the business. _____s are often favored over corporations for taxation purposes, as the _____ structure does not generally incur a tax on profits before it is distributed to the partners (i.e. there is no dividend tax levied.) However, depending on the _____ structure and the jurisdiction in which it operates, owners of a _____ may be exposed to greater personal liability than they would as shareholders of a corporation.

a. Due process
b. Federal Employers Liability Act
c. Mediation
d. Partnership

5. A _____ also known as a sole trader, or simply proprietorship is a type of business entity which there is only one owner and he has the final word taking all desicions by himself. All debts of the business are debts of the owner and must pay from his personal possessions. This means that the owner has unlimited liabilty.

a. Golden hello
b. Foreign ownership
c. Business rule
d. Sole proprietorship

6. An _____ is a comprehensive report on a company's activities throughout the preceding year. _____s are intended to give shareholders and other interested persons information about the company's activities and financial performance. Most jurisdictions require companies to prepare and disclose _____s, and many require the _____ to be filed at the company's registry.

a. A4e
b. Annual report
c. AAAI
d. A Stake in the Outcome

7. _____ is the state or fact of exclusive rights and control over property, which may be an object, land/real estate or intellectual property. An _____ right is also referred to as title. The concept of _____ has existed for thousands of years and in all cultures.

a. A4e
b. A Stake in the Outcome
c. Ownership
d. Emanation of the state

8. The term '_____' refers to the concept of collecting information and attempting to spot a pattern in the information. In some fields of study, the term '_____' has more formally-defined meanings.

In project management _____ is a mathematical technique that uses historical results to predict future outcome.

a. Trend analysis
b. Least squares
c. Stepwise regression
d. Regression analysis

9. An _____ is a mostly hierarchical concept of subordination of entities that collaborate and contribute to serve one common aim.

Organizations are a variant of clustered entities. The structure of an organization is usually set up in many a styles, dependent on their objectives and ambience.

a. Organizational development
b. Informal organization
c. Open shop
d. Organizational structure

10. _____ refers to the movement of cash into or out of a business or financial product. It is usually measured during a specified, finite period of time. Measurement of _____ can be used

- to determine a project's rate of return or value. The time of _____s into and out of projects are used as inputs in financial models such as internal rate of return, and net present value.
- to determine problems with a business's liquidity. Being profitable does not necessarily mean being liquid. A company can fail because of a shortage of cash, even while profitable.
- as an alternate measure of a business's profits when it is believed that accrual accounting concepts do not represent economic realities. For example, a company may be notionally profitable but generating little operational cash (as may be the case for a company that barters its products rather than selling for cash.) In such a case, the company may be deriving additional operating cash by issuing shares evaluating default risk, re-investment requirements, etc.

_____ is a generic term used differently depending on the context. It may be defined by users for their own purposes.

   a. Sweat equity
   b. Gross profit margin
   c. Gross profit
   d. Cash flow

11. _____ is an advertisement in which a particular product specifically mentions a competitor by name for the express purpose of showing why the competitor is inferior to the product naming it.

This should not be confused with parody advertisements, where a fictional product is being advertised for the purpose of poking fun at the particular advertisement, nor should it be confused with the use of a coined brand name for the purpose of comparing the product without actually naming an actual competitor. ('Wikipedia tastes better and is less filling than the Encyclopedia Galactica.')

In the 1980s, during what has been referred to as the cola wars, soft-drink manufacturer Pepsi ran a series of advertisements where people, caught on hidden camera, in a blind taste test, chose Pepsi over rival Coca-Cola.

   a. 33 Strategies of War
   b. 1990 Clean Air Act
   c. Comparative advertising
   d. 28-hour day

12. _____ is the term used for a branch of public policy which encompasses various disciplines which seek to order and regulate the use of land in an efficient and ethical way.

Despite confusing nomenclature, the essential function of _____ remains the same whatever term is applied. The Canadian Institute of Planners offers a definition that: '[Land use] planning means the scientific, aesthetic, and orderly disposition of land, resources, facilities and services with a view to securing the physical, economic and social efficiency, health and well-being of urban and rural communities'

In the English speaking world, the terms _____, town and country planning, regional planning, town planning, urban planning, and urban design are often used interchangeably, and will depend on the country in question but do not always have the same meaning.

a. 1990 Clean Air Act
b. 33 Strategies of War
c. Land use planning
d. 28-hour day

Chapter 4. Leisure-Service Program Development

1. _____ is a process for determining and addressing needs, or gaps between current conditions and desired conditions organizations it is known as community needs analysis. It involves identifying material problems/deficits/weaknesses and advantages/opportunites/strengths, and evaluating possible solutions that take those qualities into consideration.
   a. 28-hour day
   b. 33 Strategies of War
   c. 1990 Clean Air Act
   d. Needs assessment

2. A _____ is a brief written statement of the purpose of a company or organization. Ideally, a _____ guides the actions of the organization, spells out its overall goal, provides a sense of direction, and guides decision making for all levels of management.

   _____s often contain the following:

   - Purpose and aim of the organization
   - The organization's primary stakeholders: clients, stockholders, etc.
   - Responsibilities of the organization toward these stakeholders
   - Products and services offered

   In developing a _____:

   - Encourage as much input as feasible from employees, volunteers, and other stakeholders
   - Publicize it broadly

   The _____ can be used to resolve differences between business stakeholders. Stakeholders include: employees including managers and executives, stockholders, board of directors, customers, suppliers, distributors, creditors, governments (local, state, federal, etc.), unions, competitors, NGO's, and the general public.

   a. 1990 Clean Air Act
   b. 28-hour day
   c. Mission statement
   d. 33 Strategies of War

3. _____ is an integrated communications-based process through which individuals and communities discover that existing and newly-identified needs and wants may be satisfied by the products and services of others.

   _____ is defined by the American _____ Association as the activity, set of institutions, and processes for creating, communicating, delivering, and exchanging offerings that have value for customers, clients, partners, and society at large. The term developed from the original meaning which referred literally to going to market, as in shopping, or going to a market to buy or sell goods or services.

a. Market development
b. Customer relationship management
c. Disruptive technology
d. Marketing

4. _____ is an advertisement in which a particular product specifically mentions a competitor by name for the express purpose of showing why the competitor is inferior to the product naming it.

This should not be confused with parody advertisements, where a fictional product is being advertised for the purpose of poking fun at the particular advertisement, nor should it be confused with the use of a coined brand name for the purpose of comparing the product without actually naming an actual competitor. ('Wikipedia tastes better and is less filling than the Encyclopedia Galactica.')

In the 1980s, during what has been referred to as the cola wars, soft-drink manufacturer Pepsi ran a series of advertisements where people, caught on hidden camera, in a blind taste test, chose Pepsi over rival Coca-Cola.

a. Comparative advertising
b. 33 Strategies of War
c. 1990 Clean Air Act
d. 28-hour day

5. A _____ is a list of the general tasks and responsibilities of a position. Typically, it also includes to whom the position reports, specifications such as the qualifications needed by the person in the job, salary range for the position, etc. A _____ is usually developed by conducting a job analysis, which includes examining the tasks and sequences of tasks necessary to perform the job.
a. Recruitment advertising
b. Recruitment Process Insourcing
c. Recruitment
d. Job description

6. A _____ is a relatively new executive level position at a corporation, company, organization typically reporting directly to the CEO or board of directors. The _____ is responsible for a brand's image, experience, and promise, and propagating it throughout all aspects of the company. The brand officer oversees marketing, advertising, design, public relations and customer service departments.
a. Purchasing manager
b. Chief executive officer
c. Chief brand officer
d. Director of communications

Chapter 4. Leisure-Service Program Development

7. In decision theory and estimation theory, the _____ of an estimator, $\hat{\theta}$, of an unknown parameter of the distribution, θ, is the expected value of the loss function

$$R(\theta, \hat{\theta}) = \mathbb{E}_\theta L(\theta, \hat{\theta}) = \int L(\theta, \hat{\theta})\, dP_\theta.$$

where dP_θ is a probability measure parametrized by θ.

- For a scalar parameter θ and a quadratic loss function,

$$L(\theta, \hat{\theta}) = (\theta - \hat{\theta})^2$$

the _____ function becomes the mean squared error of the estimate,

$$R(\theta, \hat{\theta}) = E_\theta (\theta - \hat{\theta})^2$$

- In density estimation, the unknown parameter is probability density itself. The loss function is typically chosen to be a norm in an appropriate function space. For example, for L² norm,

$$L(f, \hat{f}) = \|f - \hat{f}\|_2^2$$

the _____ function becomes the mean integrated squared error

$$R(f, \hat{f}) = E\|f - \hat{f}\|^2$$

a. Financial modeling
b. Linear model
c. Risk
d. Risk aversion

8. _____ is the identification, assessment, and prioritization of risks followed by coordinated and economical application of resources to minimize, monitor, and control the probability and/or impact of unfortunate events.. Risks can come from uncertainty in financial markets, project failures, legal liabilities, credit risk, accidents, natural causes and disasters as well as deliberate attacks from an adversary. Several _____ standards have been developed including the Project Management Institute, the National Institute of Science and Technology, actuarial societies, and ISO standards.

a. Kanban
b. Risk management
c. Succession planning
d. Trademark

9. _____ is a business management strategy aimed at embedding awareness of quality in all organizational processes. _____ has been widely used in manufacturing, education, hospitals, call centers, government, and service industries, as well as NASA space and science programs.

As defined by the International Organization for Standardization (ISO):

' _____ is a management approach for an organization, centered on quality, based on the participation of all its members and aiming at long-term success through customer satisfaction, and benefits to all members of the organization and to society.' ISO 8402:1994

One major aim is to reduce variation from every process so that greater consistency of effort is obtained. (Royse, D., Thyer, B., Padgett D., ' Logan T., 2006)

a. 28-hour day
b. 1990 Clean Air Act
c. Quality management
d. Total quality management

10. _____ can be considered to have three main components: quality control, quality assurance and quality improvement. _____ is focused not only on product quality, but also the means to achieve it. _____ therefore uses quality assurance and control of processes as well as products to achieve more consistent quality.
a. 28-hour day
b. 1990 Clean Air Act
c. Total quality management
d. Quality management

Chapter 5. Facilities Development and Maintenance

1. The 'business case for _____', theorizes that in a global marketplace, a company that employs a diverse workforce (both men and women, people of many generations, people from ethnically and racially diverse backgrounds etc.) is better able to understand the demographics of the marketplace it serves and is thus better equipped to thrive in that marketplace than a company that has a more limited range of employee demographics.

   An additional corollary suggests that a company that supports the _____ of its workforce can also improve employee satisfaction, productivity and retention.

   a. Kanban
   b. Virtual team
   c. Trademark
   d. Diversity

2. The term '_____' refers to the concept of collecting information and attempting to spot a pattern in the information. In some fields of study, the term '_____' has more formally-defined meanings.

   In project management _____ is a mathematical technique that uses historical results to predict future outcome.

   a. Trend analysis
   b. Regression analysis
   c. Stepwise regression
   d. Least squares

3. _____ is an organization's process of defining its strategy and making decisions on allocating its resources to pursue this strategy, including its capital and people. Various business analysis techniques can be used in _____, including SWOT analysis (Strengths, Weaknesses, Opportunities, and Threats) and PEST analysis (Political, Economic, Social, and Technological analysis) or STEER analysis involving Socio-cultural, Technological, Economic, Ecological, and Regulatory factors and EPISTEL (Environment, Political, Informatic, Social, Technological, Economic and Legal)

   _____ is the formal consideration of an organization's future course. All _____ deals with at least one of three key questions:

   1. 'What do we do?'
   2. 'For whom do we do it?'
   3. 'How do we excel?'

   In business _____, the third question is better phrased 'How can we beat or avoid competition?'. (Bradford and Duncan, page 1.)

Chapter 5. Facilities Development and Maintenance

a. 28-hour day
b. 1990 Clean Air Act
c. 33 Strategies of War
d. Strategic planning

4. _____ is a national organization whose mission is to 'enable all young people, especially those who need us most, to reach their full potential as productive, caring, responsible citizens.' Club programs and services promote and enhance the development of boys and girls by instilling a sense of competence, usefulness, belonging and influence.

Headquarters are located in Atlanta, with regional offices in Chicago, Dallas, Atlanta, New York City and Los Angeles.

The group holds a congressional charter under Title 36 of the United States Code.

a. Wells Fargo ' Co.
b. National Association for the Advancement of Colored People
c. National Association of Corporate Directors
d. Boys ' Girls Clubs of America

5. An _____ is a comprehensive report on a company's activities throughout the preceding year. _____s are intended to give shareholders and other interested persons information about the company's activities and financial performance. Most jurisdictions require companies to prepare and disclose _____s, and many require the _____ to be filed at the company's registry.
a. AAAI
b. A Stake in the Outcome
c. Annual report
d. A4e

6. _____ plant, and equipment, is a term used in accountancy for assets and property which cannot easily be converted into cash. This can be compared with current assets such as cash or bank accounts, which are described as liquid assets. In most cases, only tangible assets are referred to as fixed.
a. Fixed asset
b. 28-hour day
c. 33 Strategies of War
d. 1990 Clean Air Act

Chapter 5. Facilities Development and Maintenance

7. The phrase mergers and _____s refers to the aspect of corporate strategy, corporate finance and management dealing with the buying, selling and combining of different companies that can aid, finance, or help a growing company in a given industry grow rapidly without having to create another business entity.

An _____, also known as a takeover or a buyout, is the buying of one company (the 'target') by another. An _____ may be friendly or hostile.

   a. A Stake in the Outcome
   b. Acquisition
   c. A4e
   d. AAAI

8. The _____ of 1990 (ADA) is the short title of United States (Pub.L. 101-336, 104 Stat. 327, enacted July 26, 1990), codified at 42 U.S.C. Â§ 12101 et seq. It was signed into law on July 26, 1990, by President George H. W. Bush, and later amended with changes effective January 1, 2009. The ADA is a wide-ranging civil rights law that prohibits, under certain circumstances, discrimination based on disability. It affords similar protections against discrimination to Americans with disabilities as the Civil Rights Act of 1964,
   a. Equal Pay Act of 1963
   b. Americans with Disabilities Act
   c. Australian labour law
   d. Employment discrimination

9. The U.S. _____ of 1973 prohibits discrimination on the basis of disability in programs conducted by Federal agencies, in programs receiving Federal financial assistance, in Federal employment, and in the employment practices of Federal contractors. The standards for determining employment discrimination under the _____ are the same as those used in title I of the Americans with Disabilities Act.

There are four key sections of the Act.

   a. Rehabilitation Act
   b. 28-hour day
   c. 33 Strategies of War
   d. 1990 Clean Air Act

10. _____ is an advertisement in which a particular product specifically mentions a competitor by name for the express purpose of showing why the competitor is inferior to the product naming it.

Chapter 5. Facilities Development and Maintenance

This should not be confused with parody advertisements, where a fictional product is being advertised for the purpose of poking fun at the particular advertisement, nor should it be confused with the use of a coined brand name for the purpose of comparing the product without actually naming an actual competitor. ('Wikipedia tastes better and is less filling than the Encyclopedia Galactica.')

In the 1980s, during what has been referred to as the cola wars, soft-drink manufacturer Pepsi ran a series of advertisements where people, caught on hidden camera, in a blind taste test, chose Pepsi over rival Coca-Cola.

   a. 33 Strategies of War
   b. 28-hour day
   c. Comparative advertising
   d. 1990 Clean Air Act

11. _____ generally refers to a list of all planned expenses and revenues. It is a plan for saving and spending. A _____ is an important concept in microeconomics, which uses a _____ line to illustrate the trade-offs between two or more goods.
   a. Budget
   b. 1990 Clean Air Act
   c. 28-hour day
   d. 33 Strategies of War

12. A _____ is a list of the general tasks and responsibilities of a position. Typically, it also includes to whom the position reports, specifications such as the qualifications needed by the person in the job, salary range for the position, etc. A _____ is usually developed by conducting a job analysis, which includes examining the tasks and sequences of tasks necessary to perform the job.
   a. Recruitment Process Insourcing
   b. Job description
   c. Recruitment advertising
   d. Recruitment

13. _____ has the following meanings:

Chapter 5. Facilities Development and Maintenance

The care and servicing by personnel for the purpose of maintaining equipment and facilities in satisfactory operating condition by providing for systematic inspection, detection, and correction of incipient failures either before they occur or before they develop into major defects.

1. Maintenance, including tests, measurements, adjustments, and parts replacement, performed specifically to prevent faults from occurring.

While _____ is generally considered to be worthwhile, there are risks such as equipment failure or human error involved when performing _____, just as in any maintenance operation. _____ as scheduled overhaul or scheduled replacement provides two of the three proactive failure management policies available to the maintenance engineer. Common methods of determining what _____ failure management policies should be applied are; OEM recommendations, requirements of codes and legislation within a jurisdiction, what an 'expert' thinks ought to be done, or the maintenance that's already done to similar equipment.

a. 33 Strategies of War
b. 28-hour day
c. 1990 Clean Air Act
d. Preventive maintenance

14. A _____ is a type of business entity in which partners (owners) share with each other the profits or losses of the business. _____s are often favored over corporations for taxation purposes, as the _____ structure does not generally incur a tax on profits before it is distributed to the partners (i.e. there is no dividend tax levied.) However, depending on the _____ structure and the jurisdiction in which it operates, owners of a _____ may be exposed to greater personal liability than they would as shareholders of a corporation.

a. Federal Employers Liability Act
b. Due process
c. Mediation
d. Partnership

Chapter 6. Creative Fiscal Management

1. _____ generally refers to a list of all planned expenses and revenues. It is a plan for saving and spending. A _____ is an important concept in microeconomics, which uses a _____ line to illustrate the trade-offs between two or more goods.
   a. 1990 Clean Air Act
   b. 28-hour day
   c. 33 Strategies of War
   d. Budget

2. _____ is the planning process used to determine whether a firm's long term investments such as new machinery, replacement machinery, new plants, new products, and research development projects are worth pursuing. It is budget for major capital, or investment, expenditures.

   Many formal methods are used in _____, including the techniques such as

   - Net present value
   - Profitability index
   - Internal rate of return
   - Modified Internal Rate of Return
   - Equivalent annuity

   These methods use the incremental cash flows from each potential investment, or project. Techniques based on accounting earnings and accounting rules are sometimes used - though economists consider this to be improper - such as the accounting rate of return, and 'return on investment.' Simplified and hybrid methods are used as well, such as payback period and discounted payback period.

   a. Gross profit
   b. Restricted stock
   c. Gross profit margin
   d. Capital budgeting

3. An _____ is the annual budget of an activity stated in terms of Budget Classification Code, functional/subfunctional categories and cost accounts. It contains estimates of the total value of resources required for the performance of the operation including reimbursable work or services for others. It also includes estimates of workload in terms of total work units identified by cost accounts.
   a. Inflation rate
   b. Operating budget
   c. Expected gain
   d. Expected return

Chapter 6. Creative Fiscal Management

4. _____ refers to the movement of cash into or out of a business or financial product. It is usually measured during a specified, finite period of time. Measurement of _____ can be used

- to determine a project's rate of return or value. The time of _____s into and out of projects are used as inputs in financial models such as internal rate of return, and net present value.
- to determine problems with a business's liquidity. Being profitable does not necessarily mean being liquid. A company can fail because of a shortage of cash, even while profitable.
- as an alternate measure of a business's profits when it is believed that accrual accounting concepts do not represent economic realities. For example, a company may be notionally profitable but generating little operational cash (as may be the case for a company that barters its products rather than selling for cash.) In such a case, the company may be deriving additional operating cash by issuing shares evaluating default risk, re-investment requirements, etc.

_____ is a generic term used differently depending on the context. It may be defined by users for their own purposes.

a. Sweat equity
b. Gross profit
c. Gross profit margin
d. Cash flow

5. _____ is an advertisement in which a particular product specifically mentions a competitor by name for the express purpose of showing why the competitor is inferior to the product naming it.

This should not be confused with parody advertisements, where a fictional product is being advertised for the purpose of poking fun at the particular advertisement, nor should it be confused with the use of a coined brand name for the purpose of comparing the product without actually naming an actual competitor. ('Wikipedia tastes better and is less filling than the Encyclopedia Galactica.')

In the 1980s, during what has been referred to as the cola wars, soft-drink manufacturer Pepsi ran a series of advertisements where people, caught on hidden camera, in a blind taste test, chose Pepsi over rival Coca-Cola.

a. 1990 Clean Air Act
b. Comparative advertising
c. 28-hour day
d. 33 Strategies of War

6. _____ is a term that refers both to:

- a formal discipline used to help appraise, or assess, the case for a project or proposal, which itself is a process known as project appraisal; and
- an informal approach to making decisions of any kind.

Chapter 6. Creative Fiscal Management 29

Under both definitions the process involves, whether explicitly or implicitly, weighing the total expected costs against the total expected benefits of one or more actions in order to choose the best or most profitable option. The formal process is often referred to as either CBA (_____) or BCost-benefit analysis

A hallmark of CBA is that all benefits and all costs are expressed in money terms, and are adjusted for the time value of money, so that all flows of benefits and flows of project costs over time (which tend to occur at different points in time) are expressed on a common basis in terms of their 'present value.' Closely related, but slightly different, formal techniques include Cost-effectiveness analysis, Economic impact analysis, Fiscal impact analysis and Social Return on Investment(SROI) analysis. The latter builds upon the logic of _____, but differs in that it is explicitly designed to inform the practical decision-making of enterprise managers and investors focused on optimising their social and environmental impacts.

   a. Gittins index
   b. Cost-benefit analysis
   c. Kepner-Tregoe
   d. Decision engineering

7. A _____ is a subset of the overall internal controls of a business covering the application of people, documents, technologies, and procedures by management accountants to solving business problems such as costing a product, service or a business-wide strategy. _____s are distinct from regular information systems in that they are used to analyze other information systems applied in operational activities in the organization. Academically, the term is commonly used to refer to the group of information management methods tied to the automation or support of human decision making, e.g. Decision Support Systems, Expert systems, and Executive information systems.
   a. 1990 Clean Air Act
   b. 28-hour day
   c. Strategic information system
   d. Management information system

8. The term '_____' refers to the concept of collecting information and attempting to spot a pattern in the information. In some fields of study, the term '_____' has more formally-defined meanings.

In project management _____ is a mathematical technique that uses historical results to predict future outcome.

   a. Regression analysis
   b. Least squares
   c. Stepwise regression
   d. Trend analysis

Chapter 6. Creative Fiscal Management

9. A _____ is a type of bond that allows the issuer of the bond to retain the privilege of redeeming the bond at some point before the bond reaches the date of maturity. In other words, on the call dates, the issuer has the right, but not the obligation, to buy back the bonds from the bond holders at the call price. Technically speaking, the bonds are not really bought and held by the issuer but cancelled immediately.

   a. Callable bond
   b. 28-hour day
   c. 33 Strategies of War
   d. 1990 Clean Air Act

10. _____ is a contract between two parties, one being the employer and the other being the employee. An employee may be defined as: 'A person in the service of another under any contract of hire, express or implied, oral or written, where the employer has the power or right to control and direct the employee in the material details of how the work is to be performed.' Black's Law Dictionary page 471 (5th ed. 1979.)

    a. Employment counsellor
    b. Employment rate
    c. Exit interview
    d. Employment

11. A _____ is a common type of municipal bond in the United States that is secured by a state or local government's pledge to use legally available resources, including tax revenues, to repay bond holders.

    Most general obligation pledges at the local government level include a pledge to levy a property tax to meet debt service requirements, in which case holders of _____s have a right to compel the borrowing government to levy that tax to satisfy the local government's obligation. Because property owners are usually reluctant to risk losing their holding due to unpaid property tax bills, credit rating agencies often consider a general obligation pledge to have very strong credit quality and frequently assign them investment grade ratings.

    a. General obligation bond
    b. 33 Strategies of War
    c. 1990 Clean Air Act
    d. 28-hour day

12. _____ refers to the process of screening, and selecting qualified people for a job at an organization or firm mid- and large-size organizations and companies often retain professional recruiters or outsource some of the process to _____ agencies. External _____ is the process of attracting and selecting employees from outside the organization.

    The _____ industry has four main types of agencies: employment agencies, _____ websites and job search engines, 'headhunters' for executive and professional _____, and in-house _____.

Chapter 6. Creative Fiscal Management

a. Referral recruitment
b. Recruitment Process Outsourcing
c. Labour hire
d. Recruitment

13. In decision theory and estimation theory, the _____ of an estimator, $\hat{\theta}$, of an unknown parameter of the distribution, θ, is the expected value of the loss function

$$R(\theta, \hat{\theta}) = \mathbb{E}_\theta L(\theta, \hat{\theta}) = \int L(\theta, \hat{\theta}) \, dP_\theta.$$

where dP_θ is a probability measure parametrized by θ.

- For a scalar parameter θ and a quadratic loss function,

$$L(\theta, \hat{\theta}) = (\theta - \hat{\theta})^2$$

the _____ function becomes the mean squared error of the estimate,

$$R(\theta, \hat{\theta}) = E_\theta (\theta - \hat{\theta})^2$$

- In density estimation, the unknown parameter is probability density itself. The loss function is typically chosen to be a norm in an appropriate function space. For example, for L^2 norm,

$$L(f, \hat{f}) = \|f - \hat{f}\|_2^2$$

the _____ function becomes the mean integrated squared error

$$R(f, \hat{f}) = E\|f - \hat{f}\|^2$$

a. Financial modeling
b. Risk
c. Linear model
d. Risk aversion

Chapter 6. Creative Fiscal Management

14. _____ is a process for determining and addressing needs, or gaps between current conditions and desired conditions organizations it is known as community needs analysis. It involves identifying material problems/deficits/weaknesses and advantages/opportunites/strengths, and evaluating possible solutions that take those qualities into consideration.

   a. 28-hour day
   b. 1990 Clean Air Act
   c. 33 Strategies of War
   d. Needs assessment

15. _____ is one of the four Ps of the marketing mix. The other three aspects are product, promotion, and place. It is also a key variable in microeconomic price allocation theory.

   a. Penetration pricing
   b. Transfer pricing
   c. Price floor
   d. Pricing

16. _____ plant, and equipment, is a term used in accountancy for assets and property which cannot easily be converted into cash. This can be compared with current assets such as cash or bank accounts, which are described as liquid assets. In most cases, only tangible assets are referred to as fixed.

   a. 1990 Clean Air Act
   b. 33 Strategies of War
   c. 28-hour day
   d. Fixed asset

17. An _____ is a practitioner of accountancy, which is the measurement, disclosure or provision of assurance about financial information that helps managers, investors, tax authorities and other decision makers make resource allocation decisions.

   The word '_____' is derived from the French 'Compter' which took its origin from the Latin 'Computare'. The word was formerly written in English as 'Accomptant', but in process of time the word, which was always pronounced by dropping the 'p', became gradually changed both in pronunciation and in orthography to its present form.

   a. A4e
   b. A Stake in the Outcome
   c. AAAI
   d. Accountant

Chapter 6. Creative Fiscal Management

18. The _____ is a private, not-for-profit organization whose primary purpose is to develop generally accepted accounting principles (GAAP) within the United States in the public's interest. The Securities and Exchange Commission (SEC) designated the _____ as the organization responsible for setting accounting standards for public companies in the U.S. It was created in 1973, replacing the Committee on Accounting Procedure (CAP) and the Accounting Principles Board (APB) of the American Institute of Certified Public Accountants (AICPA.)

The _____'s mission is 'to establish and improve standards of financial accounting and reporting for the guidance and education of the public, including issuers, auditors, and users of financial information.' To achieve this, _____ has five goals:

- Improve the usefulness of financial reporting by focusing on the primary characteristics of relevance and reliability, and on the qualities of comparability and consistency.
- Keep standards current to reflect changes in methods of doing business and in the economy.
- Consider promptly any significant areas of deficiency in financial reporting that might be improved through standard setting.
- Promote international convergence of accounting standards concurrent with improving the quality of financial reporting.
- Improve common understanding of the nature and purposes of information in financial reports.

The _____ is not a governmental body. The SEC has legal authority to establish financial accounting and reporting standards for publicly held companies under the Securities Exchange Act of 1934.

   a. Foreign direct investment
   b. Prospero Business Suite
   c. Chief risk officer
   d. Financial Accounting Standards Board

19. The general definition of an _____ is an evaluation of a person, organization, system, process, project or product. _____s are performed to ascertain the validity and reliability of information; also to provide an assessment of a system's internal control. The goal of an _____ is to express an opinion on the person / organization/system (etc) in question, under evaluation based on work done on a test basis.
   a. Audit committee
   b. Internal control
   c. A Stake in the Outcome
   d. Audit

20. In financial accounting, a _____ or statement of financial position is a summary of a person's or organization's balances. Assets, liabilities and ownership equity are listed as of a specific date, such as the end of its financial year. A _____ is often described as a snapshot of a company's financial condition.

Chapter 6. Creative Fiscal Management

   a. 28-hour day
   b. 33 Strategies of War
   c. 1990 Clean Air Act
   d. Balance sheet

21. In economics, business, retail, and accounting, a _____ is the value of money that has been used up to produce something, and hence is not available for use anymore. In economics, a _____ is an alternative that is given up as a result of a decision. In business, the _____ may be one of acquisition, in which case the amount of money expended to acquire it is counted as _____.
   a. Cost allocation
   b. Fixed costs
   c. Cost overrun
   d. Cost

22. In management accounting, _____ establishes budget and actual cost of operations, processes, departments or product and the analysis of variances, profitability or social use of funds. Managers use _____ to support decision-making to cut a company's costs and improve profitability. As a form of management accounting, _____ need not follow standards such as GAAP, because its primary use is for internal managers, rather than outside users, and what to compute is instead decided pragmatically.
   a. Quality costs
   b. Transaction cost
   c. Marginal cost
   d. Cost accounting

23. An _____ is a comprehensive report on a company's activities throughout the preceding year. _____s are intended to give shareholders and other interested persons information about the company's activities and financial performance. Most jurisdictions require companies to prepare and disclose _____s, and many require the _____ to be filed at the company's registry.
   a. A Stake in the Outcome
   b. A4e
   c. AAAI
   d. Annual report

24. _____ is a national organization whose mission is to 'enable all young people, especially those who need us most, to reach their full potential as productive, caring, responsible citizens.' Club programs and services promote and enhance the development of boys and girls by instilling a sense of competence, usefulness, belonging and influence.

Chapter 6. Creative Fiscal Management 35

Headquarters are located in Atlanta, with regional offices in Chicago, Dallas, Atlanta, New York City and Los Angeles.

The group holds a congressional charter under Title 36 of the United States Code.

  a. National Association for the Advancement of Colored People
  b. National Association of Corporate Directors
  c. Wells Fargo ' Co.
  d. Boys ' Girls Clubs of America

25. _____ according to Onuoha (2007) is the practice of starting new organizations or revitalizing mature organizations, particularly new businesses generally in response to identified opportunities. _____ is often a difficult undertaking, as a vast majority of new businesses fail. Entrepreneurial activities are substantially different depending on the type of organization that is being started.
  a. A4e
  b. AAAI
  c. A Stake in the Outcome
  d. Entrepreneurship

26. _____ is an integrated communications-based process through which individuals and communities discover that existing and newly-identified needs and wants may be satisfied by the products and services of others.

_____ is defined by the American _____ Association as the activity, set of institutions, and processes for creating, communicating, delivering, and exchanging offerings that have value for customers, clients, partners, and society at large. The term developed from the original meaning which referred literally to going to market, as in shopping, or going to a market to buy or sell goods or services.

  a. Market development
  b. Customer relationship management
  c. Disruptive technology
  d. Marketing

27. _____ is the practice of managing the flow of information between an organization and its publics. _____ gains an organization or individual exposure to their audiences using topics of public interest and news items that do not require direct payment. Because _____ places exposure in credible third-party outlets, it offers a third-party legitimacy that advertising does not have.

a. 1990 Clean Air Act
b. Two-way communication
c. 28-hour day
d. Public relations

28. A _____ is a group of people or organizations sharing one or more characteristics that cause them to have similar product and/or service needs. A true _____ meets all of the following criteria: it is distinct from other segments (different segments have different needs), it is homogeneous within the segment (exhibits common needs); it responds similarly to a market stimulus, and it can be reached by a market intervention. The term is also used when consumers with identical product and/or service needs are divided up into groups so they can be charged different amounts.
   a. SWOT analysis
   b. Context analysis
   c. Customer relationship management
   d. Market segment

Chapter 7. Human Resource Management: Maximizing Staff Performance

1. _____ is the strategic and coherent approach to the management of an organisation's most valued assets - the people working there who individually and collectively contribute to the achievement of the objectives of the business. The terms '_____' and 'human resources' (HR) have largely replaced the term 'personnel management' as a description of the processes involved in managing people in organizations. In simple sense, _____ means employing people, developing their resources, utilizing, maintaining and compensating their services in tune with the job and organizational requirement.
    a. Human resource management
    b. Job knowledge
    c. Progressive discipline
    d. Revolving door syndrome

2. _____ is a contract between two parties, one being the employer and the other being the employee. An employee may be defined as: 'A person in the service of another under any contract of hire, express or implied, oral or written, where the employer has the power or right to control and direct the employee in the material details of how the work is to be performed.' Black's Law Dictionary page 471 (5th ed. 1979.)
    a. Employment counsellor
    b. Exit interview
    c. Employment
    d. Employment rate

3. A _____ is a list of the general tasks and responsibilities of a position. Typically, it also includes to whom the position reports, specifications such as the qualifications needed by the person in the job, salary range for the position, etc. A _____ is usually developed by conducting a job analysis, which includes examining the tasks and sequences of tasks necessary to perform the job.
    a. Recruitment advertising
    b. Recruitment
    c. Job description
    d. Recruitment Process Insourcing

4. _____ is the use of empirically demonstrated behavior change techniques to improve behavior, such as altering an individual's behaviors and reactions to stimuli through positive and negative reinforcement of adaptive behavior and/or the reduction of maladaptive behavior through punishment and/or therapy.

    The first use of the term _____ appears to have been by Edward Thorndike in 1911

    a. 28-hour day
    b. 1990 Clean Air Act
    c. 33 Strategies of War
    d. Behavior modification

Chapter 7. Human Resource Management: Maximizing Staff Performance

5. _____ is an advertisement in which a particular product specifically mentions a competitor by name for the express purpose of showing why the competitor is inferior to the product naming it.

This should not be confused with parody advertisements, where a fictional product is being advertised for the purpose of poking fun at the particular advertisement, nor should it be confused with the use of a coined brand name for the purpose of comparing the product without actually naming an actual competitor. ('Wikipedia tastes better and is less filling than the Encyclopedia Galactica.')

In the 1980s, during what has been referred to as the cola wars, soft-drink manufacturer Pepsi ran a series of advertisements where people, caught on hidden camera, in a blind taste test, chose Pepsi over rival Coca-Cola.

a. 28-hour day
b. 1990 Clean Air Act
c. 33 Strategies of War
d. Comparative advertising

6. _____ refers to the process of screening, and selecting qualified people for a job at an organization or firm mid- and large-size organizations and companies often retain professional recruiters or outsource some of the process to _____ agencies. External _____ is the process of attracting and selecting employees from outside the organization.

The _____ industry has four main types of agencies: employment agencies, _____ websites and job search engines, 'headhunters' for executive and professional _____, and in-house _____.

a. Recruitment Process Outsourcing
b. Labour hire
c. Referral recruitment
d. Recruitment

7. _____ is a form of communication that typically attempts to persuade potential customers to purchase or to consume more of a particular brand of product or service. 'While now central to the contemporary global economy and the reproduction of global production networks, it is only quite recently that _____ has been more than a marginal influence on patterns of sales and production. The formation of modern _____ was intimately bound up with the emergence of new forms of monopoly capitalism around the end of the 19th and beginning of the 20th century as one element in corporate strategies to create, organize and where possible control markets, especially for mass produced consumer goods.

a. AAAI
b. Advertising
c. A Stake in the Outcome
d. A4e

Chapter 7. Human Resource Management: Maximizing Staff Performance   39

8. _____ is a national organization whose mission is to 'enable all young people, especially those who need us most, to reach their full potential as productive, caring, responsible citizens.' Club programs and services promote and enhance the development of boys and girls by instilling a sense of competence, usefulness, belonging and influence.

Headquarters are located in Atlanta, with regional offices in Chicago, Dallas, Atlanta, New York City and Los Angeles.

The group holds a congressional charter under Title 36 of the United States Code.

   a. National Association for the Advancement of Colored People
   b. Wells Fargo ' Co.
   c. National Association of Corporate Directors
   d. Boys ' Girls Clubs of America

9. The term _____ was created by President Lyndon B. Johnson when he signed Executive Order 11246 on September 24, 1965, created to prohibit federal contractors from discriminating against employees on the basis of race, sex, creed, religion, color, or national origin. In more recent times, most employers have also added sexual orientation to the list of non-discrimination.

The Executive Order also required contractors to implement affirmative action plans to increase the participation of minorities and women in the workplace.

   a. Equal employment opportunity
   b. AAAI
   c. A4e
   d. A Stake in the Outcome

10. _____ is unwelcome harassment of a sexual nature, or based upon the receiving party's sex or gender. In some contexts or circumstances, _____ may be illegal. It includes a range of behavior from seemingly mild transgressions and annoyances to actual sexual abuse or sexual assault.
   a. Hypernorms
   b. 1990 Clean Air Act
   c. 28-hour day
   d. Sexual harassment

11. An _____ is a comprehensive report on a company's activities throughout the preceding year. _____s are intended to give shareholders and other interested persons information about the company's activities and financial performance. Most jurisdictions require companies to prepare and disclose _____s, and many require the _____ to be filed at the company's registry.

a. AAAI
b. Annual report
c. A Stake in the Outcome
d. A4e

12. _____ is an all encompassing term within a broad spectrum of post-secondary learning activities and programs. The term is used mainly in the United States. Recognized forms of post-secondary learning activities within the domain include: degree credit courses by non-traditional students, non-degree career training, workforce training, formal personal enrichment courses (both on-campus and online) self-directed learning (such as through Internet interest groups, clubs or personal research activities) and experiential learning as applied to problem solving.
a. 28-hour day
b. 33 Strategies of War
c. 1990 Clean Air Act
d. Continuing education

13. Human resource management (HRM) is the strategic and coherent approach to the management of an organisation's most valued assets - the people working there who individually and collectively contribute to the achievement of the objectives of the business. The terms 'human resource management' and 'human resources' (HR) have largely replaced the term '_____' as a description of the processes involved in managing people in organizations. In simple sense, HRM means employing people, developing their resources, utilizing, maintaining and compensating their services in tune with the job and organizational requirement.
a. Personnel management
b. Salary
c. Human resources
d. Progressive discipline

14. A _____ is a relatively new executive level position at a corporation, company, organization typically reporting directly to the CEO or board of directors. The _____ is responsible for a brand's image, experience, and promise, and propagating it throughout all aspects of the company. The brand officer oversees marketing, advertising, design, public relations and customer service departments.
a. Chief executive officer
b. Director of communications
c. Purchasing manager
d. Chief brand officer

15. A _____ is typically described as a deliberate plan of action to guide decisions and achieve rational outcome(s). However, the term may also be used to denote what is actually done, even though it is unplanned.

Chapter 7. Human Resource Management: Maximizing Staff Performance   41

The term may apply to government, private sector organizations and groups, and individuals.

a. 28-hour day
b. 33 Strategies of War
c. 1990 Clean Air Act
d. Policy

16. _____ is a term defined by the Oxford English Dictionary as an individual's 'course or progress through life '. It is usually considered to pertain to remunerative work (and sometimes also formal education.)

The etymology of the term is somewhat ironic in that it comes from the Latin word carrera, which means race .

a. Nursing shortage
b. Spatial mismatch
c. Career planning
d. Career

17. In organizational development (or OD), the study of _____ looks at:

- how individuals manage their careers within and between organizations
- and how organizations structure the career progress of their members, it can also be tied into succession planning within some organizations.

In personal development, _____ is:

- ' ... the total constellation of psychological, sociological, educational, physical, economic, and chance factors that combine to influence the nature and significance of work in the total lifespan of any given individual.'

- '... the lifelong psychological and behavioral processes as well as contextual influences shaping one's career over the life span. As such, _____ involves the person's creation of a career pattern, decision-making style, integration of life roles, values expression, and life-role self concepts.'

Figures in _____

- Jeff A. Brown
- Jesse B. Davis
- Caela Farren
- John L. Holland
- Kris Magnusson
- Frank Parsons
- Vance Peavy
- Edgar Schein
- Rino Schreuder
- Mark L. Savickas
- Donald Super

a. Business process reengineering
b. Sole proprietorship
c. Horizontal integration
d. Career development

18. A _____ is a type of business entity in which partners (owners) share with each other the profits or losses of the business. _____s are often favored over corporations for taxation purposes, as the _____ structure does not generally incur a tax on profits before it is distributed to the partners (i.e. there is no dividend tax levied.) However, depending on the _____ structure and the jurisdiction in which it operates, owners of a _____ may be exposed to greater personal liability than they would as shareholders of a corporation.
 a. Mediation
 b. Due process
 c. Partnership
 d. Federal Employers Liability Act

19. In neuroscience, the _____ is a collection of brain structures which attempts to regulate and control behavior by inducing pleasurable effects.

A psychological reward is a process that reinforces behavior -- something that, when offered, causes a behavior to increase in intensity. Reward is an operational concept for describing the positive value an individual ascribes to an object, behavioral act or an internal physical state.

Chapter 7. Human Resource Management: Maximizing Staff Performance

a. 33 Strategies of War
b. 28-hour day
c. 1990 Clean Air Act
d. Reward system

20. The 'business case for _____', theorizes that in a global marketplace, a company that employs a diverse workforce (both men and women, people of many generations, people from ethnically and racially diverse backgrounds etc.) is better able to understand the demographics of the marketplace it serves and is thus better equipped to thrive in that marketplace than a company that has a more limited range of employee demographics.

An additional corollary suggests that a company that supports the _____ of its workforce can also improve employee satisfaction, productivity and retention.

a. Kanban
b. Virtual team
c. Trademark
d. Diversity

21. _____ is training for the purpose of increasing participants' cultural awareness, knowledge, and skills, which is based on the assumption that the training will benefit an organization by protecting against civil rights violations, increasing the inclusion of different identity groups, and promoting better teamwork.

_____ has been a controversial issue, due to moral considerations as well as questioned efficiency or even counterproductivity.

According to Michael Bird, many project managers may feel that they are treading new territory as they lead project teams made of individuals from different cultures, heterogeneous mixes, and differing demographics.

a. Role conflict
b. Soft skill
c. Diversity training
d. Self-disclosure

22. _____ can be regarded as an outcome of mental processes (cognitive process) leading to the selection of a course of action among several alternatives. Every _____ process produces a final choice. The output can be an action or an opinion of choice.

a. 33 Strategies of War
b. 28-hour day
c. 1990 Clean Air Act
d. Decision making

23. _____ is a group creativity technique designed to generate a large number of ideas for the solution of a problem. The method was first popularized in the late 1930s by Alex Faickney Osborn in a book called Applied Imagination. Osborn proposed that groups could double their creative output with _____.
a. Affiliation
b. Abraham Harold Maslow
c. Adam Smith
d. Brainstorming

24. _____ is a range of processes aimed at alleviating or eliminating sources of conflict. The term '_____' is sometimes used interchangeably with the term dispute resolution or alternative dispute resolution. Processes of _____ generally include negotiation, mediation and diplomacy.
a. 1990 Clean Air Act
b. 33 Strategies of War
c. 28-hour day
d. Conflict resolution

25. The field of _____ looks at the relationship between management and workers, particularly groups of workers represented by a union.

_____ is an important factor in analyzing 'varieties of capitalism', such as neocorporatism, social democracy, and neoliberalism

a. Organizational effectiveness
b. Overtime
c. Industrial relations
d. Informal organization

26. A _____ or labor union is an organization of workers who have banded together to achieve common goals in key areas and working conditions. The _____, through its leadership, bargains with the employer on behalf of union members (rank and file members) and negotiates labor contracts (Collective bargaining) with employers. This may include the negotiation of wages, work rules, complaint procedures, rules governing hiring, firing and promotion of workers, benefits, workplace safety and policies.

a. Company union
b. Trade union
c. Working time
d. Labour law

Chapter 8. Public and Community Relations: Growing Use of Partnerships

1. _____ is the practice of managing the flow of information between an organization and its publics. _____ gains an organization or individual exposure to their audiences using topics of public interest and news items that do not require direct payment. Because _____ places exposure in credible third-party outlets, it offers a third-party legitimacy that advertising does not have.
   a. Two-way communication
   b. 28-hour day
   c. 1990 Clean Air Act
   d. Public relations

2. _____ is the pursuit of influencing outcomes -- including public-policy and resource allocation decisions within political, economic, and social systems and institutions -- that directly affect people's current lives. (Cohen, 2001)

   Therefore, _____ can be seen as a deliberate process of speaking out on issues of concern in order to exert some influence on behalf of ideas or persons. Based on this definition, Cohen (2001) states that 'ideologues of all persuasions advocate' to bring a change in people's lives.

   a. Advocacy
   b. AAAI
   c. A4e
   d. A Stake in the Outcome

3. A _____ is a relatively new executive level position at a corporation, company, organization typically reporting directly to the CEO or board of directors. The _____ is responsible for a brand's image, experience, and promise, and propagating it throughout all aspects of the company. The brand officer oversees marketing, advertising, design, public relations and customer service departments.
   a. Chief brand officer
   b. Chief executive officer
   c. Director of communications
   d. Purchasing manager

4. An _____ is a comprehensive report on a company's activities throughout the preceding year. _____s are intended to give shareholders and other interested persons information about the company's activities and financial performance. Most jurisdictions require companies to prepare and disclose _____s, and many require the _____ to be filed at the company's registry.
   a. Annual report
   b. A Stake in the Outcome
   c. AAAI
   d. A4e

Chapter 8. Public and Community Relations: Growing Use of Partnerships   47

5. _____ is a national organization whose mission is to 'enable all young people, especially those who need us most, to reach their full potential as productive, caring, responsible citizens.' Club programs and services promote and enhance the development of boys and girls by instilling a sense of competence, usefulness, belonging and influence.

Headquarters are located in Atlanta, with regional offices in Chicago, Dallas, Atlanta, New York City and Los Angeles.

The group holds a congressional charter under Title 36 of the United States Code.

  a. Wells Fargo ' Co.
  b. National Association for the Advancement of Colored People
  c. National Association of Corporate Directors
  d. Boys ' Girls Clubs of America

6. A _____ is typically described as a deliberate plan of action to guide decisions and achieve rational outcome(s.) However, the term may also be used to denote what is actually done, even though it is unplanned.

The term may apply to government, private sector organizations and groups, and individuals.

  a. 33 Strategies of War
  b. Policy
  c. 28-hour day
  d. 1990 Clean Air Act

7. A _____ is a type of business entity in which partners (owners) share with each other the profits or losses of the business. _____s are often favored over corporations for taxation purposes, as the _____ structure does not generally incur a tax on profits before it is distributed to the partners (i.e. there is no dividend tax levied.) However, depending on the _____ structure and the jurisdiction in which it operates, owners of a _____ may be exposed to greater personal liability than they would as shareholders of a corporation.
  a. Federal Employers Liability Act
  b. Partnership
  c. Due process
  d. Mediation

8. The term '_____' refers to the concept of collecting information and attempting to spot a pattern in the information. In some fields of study, the term '_____' has more formally-defined meanings.

In project management _____ is a mathematical technique that uses historical results to predict future outcome.

a. Stepwise regression
b. Regression analysis
c. Least squares
d. Trend analysis

9. _____ is the incidence or process of transferring ownership of a business, enterprise, agency or public service from the public sector (government) to the private sector (business.) In a broader sense, _____ refers to transfer of any government function to the private sector including governmental functions like revenue collection and law enforcement.
a. 28-hour day
b. 1990 Clean Air Act
c. Performance reports
d. Privatization

Chapter 9. Leisure Services and the Law: Risk-Management Concerns

1. In decision theory and estimation theory, the _____ of an estimator, $\hat{\theta}$, of an unknown parameter of the distribution, θ, is the expected value of the loss function

$$R(\theta, \hat{\theta}) = \mathbb{E}_\theta L(\theta, \hat{\theta}) = \int L(\theta, \hat{\theta}) \, dP_\theta.$$

where dP_θ is a probability measure parametrized by θ.

- For a scalar parameter θ and a quadratic loss function,

$$L(\theta, \hat{\theta}) = (\theta - \hat{\theta})^2$$

the _____ function becomes the mean squared error of the estimate,

$$R(\theta, \hat{\theta}) = E_\theta (\theta - \hat{\theta})^2$$

- In density estimation, the unknown parameter is probability density itself. The loss function is typically chosen to be a norm in an appropriate function space. For example, for L^2 norm,

$$L(f, \hat{f}) = \|f - \hat{f}\|_2^2$$

the _____ function becomes the mean integrated squared error

$$R(f, \hat{f}) = E\|f - \hat{f}\|^2$$

a. Linear model
b. Financial modeling
c. Risk
d. Risk aversion

2. _____ is an advertisement in which a particular product specifically mentions a competitor by name for the express purpose of showing why the competitor is inferior to the product naming it.

This should not be confused with parody advertisements, where a fictional product is being advertised for the purpose of poking fun at the particular advertisement, nor should it be confused with the use of a coined brand name for the purpose of comparing the product without actually naming an actual competitor. ('Wikipedia tastes better and is less filling than the Encyclopedia Galactica.')

Chapter 9. Leisure Services and the Law: Risk-Management Concerns

In the 1980s, during what has been referred to as the cola wars, soft-drink manufacturer Pepsi ran a series of advertisements where people, caught on hidden camera, in a blind taste test, chose Pepsi over rival Coca-Cola.

a. 33 Strategies of War
b. 1990 Clean Air Act
c. Comparative advertising
d. 28-hour day

3. _____ is a legal concept in the common law legal systems usually used to achieve compensation for injuries (not accidents.) _____ is a type of tort or delict (also known as a civil wrong.)
   a. Certificate of Incorporation
   b. Mediation
   c. Negligence
   d. Diminishing returns

4. Under the _____ doctrine of the law of torts, a landowner may be held liable for injuries to children trespassing on the land if the injury is caused by a hazardous object or condition on the land that is likely to attract children who are unable to appreciate the risk posed by the object or condition. The doctrine has been applied to hold landowners liable for injuries caused by abandoned cars, piles of lumber or sand, trampolines, and swimming pools. However, it can be applied to virtually anything on the property of the landowner.
   a. Equal Pay Act
   b. Unreported employment
   c. Oncale v. Sundowner Offshore Services
   d. Attractive nuisance

5. _____ is a partial legal defense that reduces the amount of damages that a plaintiff can recover in a negligence-based claim based upon the degree to which the plaintiff's own negligence contributed to cause the injury. When the defense is asserted, the fact-finder, usually a jury, must decide the degree to which the plaintiff's negligence versus the combined negligence of all other relevant actors contributed to cause the plaintiff's damages. It is a modification of the doctrine of contributory negligence which disallows any recovery by a plaintiff whose negligence contributed, even minimally, to causing the damages.
   a. Joint venture
   b. Comparative negligence
   c. Bylaw
   d. Food, Drug, and Cosmetic Act

Chapter 9. Leisure Services and the Law: Risk-Management Concerns

6. _____ is a common law defense to a claim based on negligence, an action in tort. It applies to cases where a plaintiff has, through his own negligence, contributed to the harm he suffered. For example, a pedestrian crosses a road negligently and is hit by a driver who was driving negligently.

   a. Contributory negligence
   b. Last Injurious Exposure Rule
   c. Sarbanes-Oxley Act
   d. Clean Water Act

7. _____ is a contract between two parties, one being the employer and the other being the employee. An employee may be defined as: 'A person in the service of another under any contract of hire, express or implied, oral or written, where the employer has the power or right to control and direct the employee in the material details of how the work is to be performed.' Black's Law Dictionary page 471 (5th ed. 1979.)

   a. Employment rate
   b. Exit interview
   c. Employment
   d. Employment counsellor

8. _____ is the use of empirically demonstrated behavior change techniques to improve behavior, such as altering an individual's behaviors and reactions to stimuli through positive and negative reinforcement of adaptive behavior and/or the reduction of maladaptive behavior through punishment and/or therapy.

   The first use of the term _____ appears to have been by Edward Thorndike in 1911

   a. 1990 Clean Air Act
   b. Behavior modification
   c. 33 Strategies of War
   d. 28-hour day

9. _____ involves establishing specific, measurable and time-targeted objectives. Work on the theory of goal-setting suggests that it's an effective tool for making progress by ensuring that participants in a group with a common goal are clearly aware of what is expected from them if an objective is to be achieved. On a personal level, setting goals is a process that allows people to specify then work towards their own objectives - most commonly with financial or career-based goals.

   a. Digital strategy
   b. Goal setting
   c. Resource-based view
   d. Catfish effect

Chapter 9. Leisure Services and the Law: Risk-Management Concerns

10. _____ is unwelcome harassment of a sexual nature, or based upon the receiving party's sex or gender. In some contexts or circumstances, _____ may be illegal. It includes a range of behavior from seemingly mild transgressions and annoyances to actual sexual abuse or sexual assault.
    a. 1990 Clean Air Act
    b. 28-hour day
    c. Hypernorms
    d. Sexual harassment

11. _____ is one of the managerial functions like planning, organizing, staffing and directing. It is an important function because it helps to check the errors and to take the corrective action so that deviation from standards are minimized and stated goals of the organization are achieved in desired manner. According to modern concepts, _____ is a foreseeing action whereas earlier concept of _____ was used only when errors were detected. _____ in management means setting standards, measuring actual performance and taking corrective action.
    a. Turnover
    b. Decision tree pruning
    c. Control
    d. Schedule of reinforcement

12. The _____ was a landmark piece of legislation in the United States that outlawed racial segregation in schools, public places, and employment.
    a. Design patent
    b. Financial Security Law of France
    c. Negligence in employment
    d. Civil Rights Act of 1964

13. _____ is the strategic and coherent approach to the management of an organisation's most valued assets - the people working there who individually and collectively contribute to the achievement of the objectives of the business. The terms '_____' and 'human resources' (HR) have largely replaced the term 'personnel management' as a description of the processes involved in managing people in organizations. In simple sense, _____ means employing people, developing their resources, utilizing, maintaining and compensating their services in tune with the job and organizational requirement.
    a. Job knowledge
    b. Revolving door syndrome
    c. Progressive discipline
    d. Human resource management

14. The field of _____ looks at the relationship between management and workers, particularly groups of workers represented by a union.

Chapter 9. Leisure Services and the Law: Risk-Management Concerns

_____ is an important factor in analyzing 'varieties of capitalism', such as neocorporatism, social democracy, and neoliberalism

a. Informal organization
b. Industrial relations
c. Overtime
d. Organizational effectiveness

15. _____ are conventions, treaties and recommendations designed to eliminate unjust and inhumane labour practices. The primary inernational agency charged with developing such standards is the International Labour Organization (ILO.) Established in 1919, the ILO advocates international standards as essential for the eradication of labour conditions involving 'injustice, hardship and privation'.

a. Airbus SAS
b. Airbus Industrie
c. Anaconda Copper
d. International labour standards

16. A _____ or labor union is an organization of workers who have banded together to achieve common goals in key areas and working conditions. The _____, through its leadership, bargains with the employer on behalf of union members (rank and file members) and negotiates labor contracts (Collective bargaining) with employers. This may include the negotiation of wages, work rules, complaint procedures, rules governing hiring, firing and promotion of workers, benefits, workplace safety and policies.

a. Working time
b. Labour law
c. Company union
d. Trade union

17. _____ is an all encompassing term within a broad spectrum of post-secondary learning activities and programs. The term is used mainly in the United States. Recognized forms of post-secondary learning activities within the domain include: degree credit courses by non-traditional students, non-degree career training, workforce training, formal personal enrichment courses (both on-campus and online) self-directed learning (such as through Internet interest groups, clubs or personal research activities) and experiential learning as applied to problem solving.

a. 33 Strategies of War
b. Continuing education
c. 1990 Clean Air Act
d. 28-hour day

Chapter 9. Leisure Services and the Law: Risk-Management Concerns

18. _____ is a term defined by the Oxford English Dictionary as an individual's 'course or progress through life '. It is usually considered to pertain to remunerative work (and sometimes also formal education.)

The etymology of the term is somewhat ironic in that it comes from the Latin word carrera, which means race .

a. Nursing shortage
b. Career
c. Career planning
d. Spatial mismatch

19. In organizational development (or OD), the study of _____ looks at:

- how individuals manage their careers within and between organizations
- and how organizations structure the career progress of their members, it can also be tied into succession planning within some organizations.

In personal development, _____ is:

- ' ... the total constellation of psychological, sociological, educational, physical, economic, and chance factors that combine to influence the nature and significance of work in the total lifespan of any given individual.'

- '... the lifelong psychological and behavioral processes as well as contextual influences shaping one's career over the life span. As such, _____ involves the person's creation of a career pattern, decision-making style, integration of life roles, values expression, and life-role self concepts.'

Figures in _____

- Jeff A. Brown
- Jesse B. Davis
- Caela Farren
- John L. Holland
- Kris Magnusson
- Frank Parsons
- Vance Peavy
- Edgar Schein
- Rino Schreuder
- Mark L. Savickas
- Donald Super

a. Sole proprietorship
b. Career development
c. Business process reengineering
d. Horizontal integration

20. A _____ is a type of business entity in which partners (owners) share with each other the profits or losses of the business. _____s are often favored over corporations for taxation purposes, as the _____ structure does not generally incur a tax on profits before it is distributed to the partners (i.e. there is no dividend tax levied.) However, depending on the _____ structure and the jurisdiction in which it operates, owners of a _____ may be exposed to greater personal liability than they would as shareholders of a corporation.
   a. Mediation
   b. Due process
   c. Partnership
   d. Federal Employers Liability Act

21. _____ plant, and equipment, is a term used in accountancy for assets and property which cannot easily be converted into cash. This can be compared with current assets such as cash or bank accounts, which are described as liquid assets. In most cases, only tangible assets are referred to as fixed.
   a. 33 Strategies of War
   b. 1990 Clean Air Act
   c. 28-hour day
   d. Fixed asset

Chapter 10. The Controlling Function

1. A _____ is a subset of the overall internal controls of a business covering the application of people, documents, technologies, and procedures by management accountants to solving business problems such as costing a product, service or a business-wide strategy. _____s are distinct from regular information systems in that they are used to analyze other information systems applied in operational activities in the organization. Academically, the term is commonly used to refer to the group of information management methods tied to the automation or support of human decision making, e.g. Decision Support Systems, Expert systems, and Executive information systems.
   a. Management information system
   b. Strategic information system
   c. 1990 Clean Air Act
   d. 28-hour day

2. _____ of the learning curve effect and the closely related experience curve effect express the relationship between equations for experience and efficiency or between efficiency gains and investment in the effort. The experience of 'learning curves' was first observed by the 19th Century German psychologist Hermann Ebbinghaus according to the difficulty of memorizing varying numbers of verbal stimuli, and subsequent learning about the complex processes of learning are discussed in the

   The rule used for representing the learning curve effect states that the more times a task has been performed, the less time will be required on each subsequent iteration.

   a. Point biserial correlation coefficient
   b. Distribution
   c. Models
   d. Spatial Decision Support Systems

3. _____ is a type of evaluation which has the purpose of improving programs. It goes under other names such as developmental evaluation and implementation evaluation. It can be contrasted with other types of evaluation which have other purposes, in particular process evaluation and outcome evaluation.
   a. 1990 Clean Air Act
   b. Risk assessment
   c. Formative evaluation
   d. 28-hour day

4. _____ refers to the assessment of the learning and summarizes the development of learners at a particular time. After a period of work, e.g. a unit for two weeks, the learner sits for a test and then the teacher marks the test and assigns a score. The test aims to summarize learning up to that point.

Chapter 10. The Controlling Function

a. Stanine
b. 28-hour day
c. Summative assessment
d. 1990 Clean Air Act

5. _____ is a civil designation for persons who are incorporated in a fixed or permanent way to a society or group: regular member of the working staff, permanent staff distinguished from a supernumerary.

The term '_____' and its counterpart, 'supernumerary,' originated in Spanish and Latin American academy and government; it is now also used in countries all over the world, such as France, the U.S., England, Italy, etc.

There are _____ members of surgical organizations, of universities, of gastronomical associations, etc.

a. Abraham Harold Maslow
b. Adam Smith
c. Affiliation
d. Numerary

6. _____ is the use of empirically demonstrated behavior change techniques to improve behavior, such as altering an individual's behaviors and reactions to stimuli through positive and negative reinforcement of adaptive behavior and/or the reduction of maladaptive behavior through punishment and/or therapy.

The first use of the term _____ appears to have been by Edward Thorndike in 1911

a. 33 Strategies of War
b. Behavior modification
c. 1990 Clean Air Act
d. 28-hour day

7. The term '_____' refers to the concept of collecting information and attempting to spot a pattern in the information. In some fields of study, the term '_____' has more formally-defined meanings.

In project management _____ is a mathematical technique that uses historical results to predict future outcome.

a. Regression analysis
b. Least squares
c. Stepwise regression
d. Trend analysis

8. _____ is a process for determining and addressing needs, or gaps between current conditions and desired conditions organizations it is known as community needs analysis. It involves identifying material problems/deficits/weaknesses and advantages/opportunites/strengths, and evaluating possible solutions that take those qualities into consideration.
a. Needs assessment
b. 28-hour day
c. 1990 Clean Air Act
d. 33 Strategies of War

9. _____ generally refers to a list of all planned expenses and revenues. It is a plan for saving and spending. A _____ is an important concept in microeconomics, which uses a _____ line to illustrate the trade-offs between two or more goods.
a. 33 Strategies of War
b. 1990 Clean Air Act
c. 28-hour day
d. Budget

10. A _____ is a list of the general tasks and responsibilities of a position. Typically, it also includes to whom the position reports, specifications such as the qualifications needed by the person in the job, salary range for the position, etc. A _____ is usually developed by conducting a job analysis, which includes examining the tasks and sequences of tasks necessary to perform the job.
a. Recruitment Process Insourcing
b. Recruitment advertising
c. Job description
d. Recruitment

11. _____ is an advertisement in which a particular product specifically mentions a competitor by name for the express purpose of showing why the competitor is inferior to the product naming it.

This should not be confused with parody advertisements, where a fictional product is being advertised for the purpose of poking fun at the particular advertisement, nor should it be confused with the use of a coined brand name for the purpose of comparing the product without actually naming an actual competitor. ('Wikipedia tastes better and is less filling than the Encyclopedia Galactica.')

Chapter 10. The Controlling Function

In the 1980s, during what has been referred to as the cola wars, soft-drink manufacturer Pepsi ran a series of advertisements where people, caught on hidden camera, in a blind taste test, chose Pepsi over rival Coca-Cola.

a. 1990 Clean Air Act
b. Comparative advertising
c. 33 Strategies of War
d. 28-hour day

12. _____ is a term defined by the Oxford English Dictionary as an individual's 'course or progress through life '. It is usually considered to pertain to remunerative work (and sometimes also formal education.)

The etymology of the term is somewhat ironic in that it comes from the Latin word carrera, which means race .

a. Nursing shortage
b. Career
c. Spatial mismatch
d. Career planning

13. In organizational development (or OD), the study of _____ looks at:

- how individuals manage their careers within and between organizations
- and how organizations structure the career progress of their members, it can also be tied into succession planning within some organizations.

In personal development, _____ is:

- ' ... the total constellation of psychological, sociological, educational, physical, economic, and chance factors that combine to influence the nature and significance of work in the total lifespan of any given individual.'

- '... the lifelong psychological and behavioral processes as well as contextual influences shaping one's career over the life span. As such, _____ involves the person's creation of a career pattern, decision-making style, integration of life roles, values expression, and life-role self concepts.'

Figures in _____

- Jeff A. Brown
- Jesse B. Davis
- Caela Farren
- John L. Holland
- Kris Magnusson
- Frank Parsons
- Vance Peavy
- Edgar Schein
- Rino Schreuder
- Mark L. Savickas
- Donald Super

a. Horizontal integration
b. Career development
c. Business process reengineering
d. Sole proprietorship

Chapter 11. The Creative Manager: Facing the Future

1. _____ has been described as the 'process of social influence in which one person can enlist the aid and support of others in the accomplishment of a common task'. A definition more inclusive of followers comes from Alan Keith of Genentech who said '_____ is ultimately about creating a way for people to contribute to making something extraordinary happen.'

   _____ is one of the most salient aspects of the organizational context. However, defining _____ has been challenging.

   a. Situational leadership
   b. 1990 Clean Air Act
   c. 28-hour day
   d. Leadership

2. _____ was a writer, management consultant, and self-described 'social ecologist.' Widely considered to be 'the father of modern management,' his 39 books and countless scholarly and popular articles explored how humans are organized across all sectors of society--in business, government and the nonprofit world. His writings have predicted many of the major developments of the late twentieth century, including privatization and decentralization; the rise of Japan to economic world power; the decisive importance of marketing; and the emergence of the information society with its necessity of lifelong learning. In 1959, Drucker coined the term 'knowledge worker' and later in his life considered knowledge work productivity to be the next frontier of management.
   a. Peter Ferdinand Drucker
   b. Debora L. Spar
   c. Jacques Al-Salawat Nasruddin Nasser
   d. Chrissie Hynde

3. _____ refers to a range of skills, tools, and techniques used to manage time when accomplishing specific tasks, projects and goals. This set encompass a wide scope of activities, and these include planning, allocating, setting goals, delegation, analysis of time spent, monitoring, organizing, scheduling, and prioritizing. Initially _____ referred to just business or work activities, but eventually the term broadened to include personal activities also.
   a. Voice of the customer
   b. Time management
   c. Formula for Change
   d. Cash cow

4. _____ is a term defined by the Oxford English Dictionary as an individual's 'course or progress through life '. It is usually considered to pertain to remunerative work (and sometimes also formal education.)

The etymology of the term is somewhat ironic in that it comes from the Latin word carrera, which means race .

a. Career planning
b. Nursing shortage
c. Career
d. Spatial mismatch

5. In organizational development (or OD), the study of _____ looks at:

   - how individuals manage their careers within and between organizations
   - and how organizations structure the career progress of their members, it can also be tied into succession planning within some organizations.

In personal development, _____ is:

   - '... the total constellation of psychological, sociological, educational, physical, economic, and chance factors that combine to influence the nature and significance of work in the total lifespan of any given individual.'

   - '... the lifelong psychological and behavioral processes as well as contextual influences shaping one's career over the life span. As such, _____ involves the person's creation of a career pattern, decision-making style, integration of life roles, values expression, and life-role self concepts.'

Figures in _____

   - Jeff A. Brown
   - Jesse B. Davis
   - Caela Farren
   - John L. Holland
   - Kris Magnusson
   - Frank Parsons
   - Vance Peavy
   - Edgar Schein
   - Rino Schreuder
   - Mark L. Savickas
   - Donald Super

a. Business process reengineering
b. Sole proprietorship
c. Horizontal integration
d. Career development

6. _____ can be regarded as an outcome of mental processes (cognitive process) leading to the selection of a course of action among several alternatives. Every _____ process produces a final choice. The output can be an action or an opinion of choice.
   a. 33 Strategies of War
   b. 1990 Clean Air Act
   c. Decision making
   d. 28-hour day

7. _____ is a term used to describe a policy of allowing events to take their own course. The term is a French phrase literally meaning 'let do'. It is a doctrine that states that government generally should not intervene in the marketplace.
   a. Deep ecology
   b. Freedom of contract
   c. Laissez-faire
   d. Libertarian

8. Contingency leadership theory in organizational studies is a type of leadership theory, leadership style, and leadership model that presumes that different leadership styles are contingent to different situations. It is also referred as _____ ® theory although, as originally convened, the situational theory term is much more restrictive. The original situational theory argues that the best type of leadership is totally determined by the situational variables. Currently there are many styles of leadership.
   a. Situational theory
   b. Situational leadership
   c. 1990 Clean Air Act
   d. 28-hour day

9. Various _____ can be employed dependent on the culture of the business, the nature of the task, the nature of the workforce and the personality and skills of the leaders. This idea was further developed by Robert Tannenbaum and Warren H. Schmidt (1958, 1973) who argued that the style of leadership is dependent upon the prevailing circumstance; therefore leaders should exercise a range of leadership styles and should deploy them as appropriate.

An Autocratic or authoritarian manager makes all the decisions, keeping the information and decision making among the senior management.

   a. 28-hour day
   b. Management styles
   c. 1990 Clean Air Act
   d. 33 Strategies of War

Chapter 11. The Creative Manager: Facing the Future

10. The 'business case for _____', theorizes that in a global marketplace, a company that employs a diverse workforce (both men and women, people of many generations, people from ethnically and racially diverse backgrounds etc.) is better able to understand the demographics of the marketplace it serves and is thus better equipped to thrive in that marketplace than a company that has a more limited range of employee demographics.

An additional corollary suggests that a company that supports the _____ of its workforce can also improve employee satisfaction, productivity and retention.

   a. Trademark
   b. Diversity
   c. Kanban
   d. Virtual team

11. _____ refers to increasing the spiritual, political, social or economic strength of individuals and communities. It often involves the empowered developing confidence in their own capacities.

The term Human _____ covers a vast landscape of meanings, interpretations, definitions and disciplines ranging from psychology and philosophy to the highly commercialized Self-Help industry and Motivational sciences.

   a. A Stake in the Outcome
   b. Empowerment
   c. AAAI
   d. A4e

12. _____ is the use of empirically demonstrated behavior change techniques to improve behavior, such as altering an individual's behaviors and reactions to stimuli through positive and negative reinforcement of adaptive behavior and/or the reduction of maladaptive behavior through punishment and/or therapy.

The first use of the term _____ appears to have been by Edward Thorndike in 1911

   a. 28-hour day
   b. 33 Strategies of War
   c. 1990 Clean Air Act
   d. Behavior modification

13. _____ is the pursuit of influencing outcomes -- including public-policy and resource allocation decisions within political, economic, and social systems and institutions -- that directly affect people's current lives. (Cohen, 2001)

Therefore, _____ can be seen as a deliberate process of speaking out on issues of concern in order to exert some influence on behalf of ideas or persons. Based on this definition, Cohen (2001) states that 'ideologues of all persuasions advocate' to bring a change in people's lives.

   a. A Stake in the Outcome
   b. Advocacy
   c. A4e
   d. AAAI

14. _____ is an organization's process of defining its strategy and making decisions on allocating its resources to pursue this strategy, including its capital and people. Various business analysis techniques can be used in _____, including SWOT analysis (Strengths, Weaknesses, Opportunities, and Threats) and PEST analysis (Political, Economic, Social, and Technological analysis) or STEER analysis involving Socio-cultural, Technological, Economic, Ecological, and Regulatory factors and EPISTEL (Environment, Political, Informatic, Social, Technological, Economic and Legal)

_____ is the formal consideration of an organization's future course. All _____ deals with at least one of three key questions:

   1. 'What do we do?'
   2. 'For whom do we do it?'
   3. 'How do we excel?'

In business _____, the third question is better phrased 'How can we beat or avoid competition?'. (Bradford and Duncan, page 1.)

   a. Strategic planning
   b. 28-hour day
   c. 1990 Clean Air Act
   d. 33 Strategies of War

15. An _____ is a comprehensive report on a company's activities throughout the preceding year. _____s are intended to give shareholders and other interested persons information about the company's activities and financial performance. Most jurisdictions require companies to prepare and disclose _____s, and many require the _____ to be filed at the company's registry.
   a. A4e
   b. A Stake in the Outcome
   c. AAAI
   d. Annual report

16. _____ is a structured approach to transitioning individuals, teams, and organizations from a current state to a desired future state. The current definition of _____ includes both organizational _____ processes and individual _____ models, which together are used to manage the people side of change.

A number of models are available for understanding the transitioning of individuals through the phases of _____ and strengthening organizational development initiative in both government and corporate sectors.

   a. 1990 Clean Air Act
   b. 28-hour day
   c. 33 Strategies of War
   d. Change management

17. _____ is an advertisement in which a particular product specifically mentions a competitor by name for the express purpose of showing why the competitor is inferior to the product naming it.

This should not be confused with parody advertisements, where a fictional product is being advertised for the purpose of poking fun at the particular advertisement, nor should it be confused with the use of a coined brand name for the purpose of comparing the product without actually naming an actual competitor. ('Wikipedia tastes better and is less filling than the Encyclopedia Galactica.')

In the 1980s, during what has been referred to as the cola wars, soft-drink manufacturer Pepsi ran a series of advertisements where people, caught on hidden camera, in a blind taste test, chose Pepsi over rival Coca-Cola.

   a. 28-hour day
   b. 1990 Clean Air Act
   c. 33 Strategies of War
   d. Comparative advertising

ANSWER KEY

Chapter 1
1. b 2. a 3. d 4. a 5. d 6. c 7. c 8. c 9. d 10. a
11. d 12. d 13. d 14. c

Chapter 2
1. d 2. c 3. c 4. c 5. a 6. a 7. a 8. c 9. d 10. d
11. a 12. a 13. d 14. d 15. d 16. c 17. c 18. b 19. d 20. c
21. d 22. c

Chapter 3
1. a 2. d 3. b 4. d 5. d 6. b 7. c 8. a 9. d 10. d
11. c 12. c

Chapter 4
1. d 2. c 3. d 4. a 5. d 6. c 7. c 8. b 9. d 10. d

Chapter 5
1. d 2. a 3. d 4. d 5. c 6. a 7. b 8. b 9. a 10. c
11. a 12. b 13. d 14. d

Chapter 6
1. d 2. d 3. b 4. d 5. b 6. b 7. d 8. d 9. a 10. d
11. a 12. d 13. b 14. d 15. d 16. d 17. d 18. d 19. d 20. d
21. d 22. d 23. d 24. d 25. d 26. d 27. d 28. d

Chapter 7
1. a 2. c 3. c 4. d 5. d 6. d 7. b 8. d 9. a 10. d
11. b 12. d 13. a 14. d 15. d 16. d 17. d 18. c 19. d 20. d
21. c 22. d 23. d 24. d 25. c 26. b

Chapter 8
1. d 2. a 3. a 4. a 5. d 6. b 7. b 8. d 9. d

Chapter 9
1. c 2. c 3. c 4. d 5. b 6. a 7. c 8. b 9. b 10. d
11. c 12. d 13. d 14. b 15. d 16. d 17. b 18. b 19. b 20. c
21. d

Chapter 10
1. a 2. c 3. c 4. c 5. d 6. b 7. d 8. a 9. d 10. c
11. b 12. b 13. b

Chapter 11
1. d 2. a 3. b 4. c 5. d 6. c 7. c 8. b 9. b 10. b
11. b 12. d 13. b 14. a 15. d 16. d 17. d

www.ingramcontent.com/pod-product-compliance
Lightning Source LLC
Chambersburg PA
CBHW081850230426
43669CB00018B/2894